One Innocent &
Ordinary Life

Short Stories and Poems

By: Brian Wayne Maki

Contents

Copyright © 2012 by Brian Wayne Maki of Marquette, Michigan | 1st Edition

ISBN 9781468105827 | All rights reserved. | Order Books: www.mc-computerhelp.com | Printed in the USA.

The Two Trees of Meadow Grove

I remember the day I first passed Meadow Grove
My car reaching the peak of the tallest hillside
These two baby spruce trees came into full view
And were no more than a foot tall to the world
Each branch extending outward to the other.

The Spring-time sun peaked over the top branch
And I imagined them as a King and Queen
The King and Queen of Meadow Grove
Sharing a quiet life together on a grassy knoll
Protected in the arms of God's grace.

I slowly passed the heavenly image
Turning my emotions and feelings that day
Into a flourish of heartfelt forgiveness
Having witnessed something so pure
Shall live beyond my soul's final heartbeat.

One day on a trip through a wooded countryside
Some fifty years beyond my youthful ways
The glorious Fall imagery stunned my heart
As the car reached the tallest hillside view
And two grown spruce trees fulfilled my eyes.

Before me stood the King and Queen of Meadow Grove
Where two noble trees had grown peaceful and wise
Each set of branches entwined with the other
Sharing in a bond few shall ever live
Until time parts them with a gentle breeze.

September 22, 2011

A Father's One Shot

Everyone has one incredible moment in life – a moment that really defines you as a person.

I was not your average hero. I was tall and thin, rather withdrawn, and never missed a single day of high school. I liked playing trumpet in band, but never once wanted the spotlight of being in front of an audience. And the one thing I loved more than anything else was basketball, but I was only an average player – accept for shooting!

January 1988 MSHS Basketball Game

When I coached basketball for middle school children, I would always begin the season by telling them the story of the "One Shot." This story was a personal insight into my own brief, but fascinating ride, into the realms of basketball glory. I always reminded players that (if they were fortunate enough) they would live one incredible moment in their life. Maybe it would happen in a public place, in a sporting event, or life in general.

For me, it happened in basketball when I took my first shot as a senior.

Basketball has been a part of my life ever since the day my father purchased a hoop and placed it in the back yard. I have been in love with it since the day I was seven years old when I made my first basket (after six hours of trying). I was obsessed with the idea of shooting a basketball from any distance, no matter how difficult the shot. I could shoot over rooftops and from incredible distances. I knew I had the gift, the eye, the tingling in the hand, and the feeling to be a great shooter. I could even hear the crowd and feel the sweat dripping down my face. I played horrible defense, however, but I knew I could shoot.

I did this feat in the privacy of my own backyard, never realizing how many others were practicing the same thing. I believed I was alone with the basket. No matter if it snowed, rained or hailed, I kept at that dream of making the big shot, the one that would bring the crowd to its feet, and the shot that everyone would remember.

In middle school, our basketball team never won a single game. I played in very few games during those years. It did not bother me, though; I was still practicing my shots at home (even after practice). Instead, I just kept playing basketball anywhere I could to stay in touch with the game.

In high school, my basketball experience consisted mainly of playing street and pickup games. Even though I made the freshmen team, I never played more than six games. I did not make the cuts in my sophomore or junior years, either; but I just kept playing basketball anywhere I could.

During my senior year, I became the manager of the team. I practiced with the team all the time, and I could always make eight three pointers like nothing. Other players became jealous and brushed me aside. But I just kept shooting and practicing.

Then one day, three players quit the team over limited playing time. I had wondered why they were so upset – I had had no playing time. Coach Gordy LeDuc then decided to ask me to join the team. Of course I said "yes." The coach gave me the golden key to the equipment room. I still remember, to this very day, walking down the hall and picking out my own jersey (any real player's fantasy). The smell of a new jersey really got to me, and I knew something special would happen the day I put it on.

During the end of a losing season for our high school team, I suited up just like all the other players. I did the warm ups with the team and then waited it out. Eventually the final two minutes remained on the clock, and then Mr. LeDuc yelled at me to check in at the scorer's table. The minute I came onto the court, I saw the crowd and I started to sweat.

It was the first two minutes I ever played as a varsity player.

Those two minutes were worth every effort to get there. I remembered, as I played, those cold winter nights running in the dark, riding my bike hundreds of miles, the countless competition I faced in pickup games and the physical toll it took upon my body to survive. I never lost sight of my goal. This moment was proving to everyone that I belonged, that I wanted to be a winner.

The ball went out of bounce at half-court. Five seconds remained. The ball was passed to me, and even double-teamed by two tall players – I let it fly from sixty-five feet out. It was my first shot as a senior. The horn went off as the ball hovered in the air for what seemed like a day. The shot went off the glass and in; the crowd went wild. We had won the game. My sister came off the bench and tackled me, along with 300 other people who were chanting my name, over and over again. I vividly remember being pushed to the floor and seeing the image of all those faces hovering above me, jumping up and down, smiling and cheering, and some with tears.

I had become a hero and I did not know it.

I stayed after that game for over two hours, signing autographs and talking with family and friends about the incredible luck I had. That was until my father sat me down (he had never attended any of my games until that night) and wanted to talk alone.

My father began a flashback to the shot and explained something about my body motion after the ball's release. He said, "Usually the body of a player goes forward when a ball is to miss, but you were back at the other end playing defense before the ball ever went in." I gasped for air. "You knew it was good, didn't you?" He knew my secret, the one no one had mentioned that night. It was not luck, but that of skill, of practice, of sweat, of dedication. But how could he know? He never played or watched any games with me growing up.

"How do you know this?" I inquired with a tear.

"Because I know sports and I saw you do this. You did great, son," he smiled and gave me a hug.

That was the closest moment I ever had with my father. Not only had I set a school record, but also had become a hero to others and an inspiration to my own father.

This is the meaning of life – the value of which is measured by each and every single accomplishment you make, and the desire and determination to get there. The game itself is meaningless without effort, persistence and purpose, requiring a particular focus to become a winner.

The Most Hated Man Alive

I put the that shirt on again
Those black and white stripes
And laced my worn black shoes
While tightening my old black pants
Preparing for yet another battle
A game of wit, strategy, and emotion
One I am all too familiar with now:
      The player who strives
      The coach who directs
      The parent who concerns.

I find all these moments alluring
To be in the middle of a war
Is not such a bad thing.

Decisive actions must be made
As the game wears down
In front of every waiting eye
For fair play is fair play
No matter where you go
When the final whistle blows
The most hated man alive
Leaves in a quick manner
Without anyone knowing
He would do it all again.

September 9, 2011

The Sound of Crashing Waves

I cannot remember the day or year
Or if it were a lake or an ocean
I only recall hearing this sound:
The sound of crashing waves.

Peacefulness rests upon my soul
And nothing in this world satisfies
More than nature shaping our land
Like it has done a million times before.

This simple act of nature descends
Upon the eardrums every season
And it is not about nature building
It is how it becomes a part of you.

Now the world can find this, too
Not just live in dreams or visions
For you will soon come to hear:
The sound of crashing waves.

September 24, 2011

Those Slim Birch Leaves

You see a top the highest limb
A handful of slim birch leaves
Will grow together, will be one.

They had been one for many months
Through Spring's sunshine and rain
And Summer's hot days and nights.

But their lives are a shadow of dreams
A story that so many of us know and love:
The tragic and fruitful end to a beautiful life.

Once the cold breeze starts
This handful of slim birch leaves
Have no other choice but to surrender.

A few may fall upon the lowest branch
Others will blow far away in the wind
And some will lie motionless and dead.

Just like all the leaves that came before
Another season will teach us again:
There is a time to live and a time to die.

September 25, 2011

One Poetry Piece

I cannot find any more words tonight
For my tired eyes have fallen shut
And this page is dreadfully empty
As I write a poem so simple and pure.

I have dreamed for many years
To find the exact words and meaning
Something sweet, something kind
But I keep pausing in the heart of battle.

I have this picture of the perfect life
Somehow it had stumbled in my mind
And I wanted you to know right now:
That I completely and utterly love you.

I could go on for a thousand poems
Expressing my gratitude, my sentiments
But that would never equal the whole image
For one verse could never say it all.

In this thought I begin to see my heart
A part of this man continuing to grow
And the new image now takes shape:
This one poetry piece is really for you.

September 25, 2011

One Peaceful Car Ride

I had traveled far and long
And this haze landed upon the road
With the hint of Heaven moving
Through each cloud puff I passed
Sailing through in a whisper
Had taken me to a peaceful place
Suddenly a tear came to my eye
The image of a brilliant day flashed
Simple joys had blossomed like flowers
Not a scrap of fear left inside
I was winning the race of life
Through each cloud puff I passed
I felt as free as a bird in flight
Then the clearing came about
This haze moved away from the road
And I was all alone again.

November 18, 2009

Let your love flow

Now only I can make the difference
Standing in this corner alone
You see yourself changing
Against all the odds one could face
The madness of a day is ending
The belief that something beautiful
Is about to sail away from your heart
You are pulled back by gravity
By something stronger than your own being.

Now only I can make the difference
I, too, have felt loneliness and despair
When there was no reason to come home
I, too, felt lost and confused
I almost lost myself to that feeling
But you came and sheltered me
I need to live by this simple thought:
Let your love flow deep in my heart
And wrap around my mind forever.

November 9, 2009

The Art of Living

There is a time for living and a time for learning
We may hear a thousand voices telling us
To climb to the highest mountain top
And to reach beyond the stars
Way beyond the reaches of our galaxy
For anything is possible there
The Earth will always spin round and round
And our dreams will come true again and again.

There is a time for living and a time for learning
There is no greater moment to live
There is no greater moment to learn
Nothing is beyond our reach
And emotions cannot hold us back
We are bound for glory in the highest
The ride is about to begin soon
And the art of living will take us there.

November 7, 2009

A Bicycle Ride that Lasted Twenty Years

The phone rang at the house one day, while I was playing outside. It was our neighbor, Mr. Jack Dixon, asking me to come over for a chat. He lived just a few doors over, and he had some opportunity for me to consider.

I can remember walking over, wondering all the while what he would want on a nice, warm summer's afternoon day. I was only a fourteen-year-old skinny boy who could run like the wind. As I approached the door, he was standing there, with this smile upon his face.

"Hello, Brian," he said. "I wanted to ask you a question."

"Okay, Mr. Dixon," I quickly responded.

"I have a friend up on Ridge Street who needs help with the lawn. Mr. & Mrs. Wilmer are looking for a young man like you to help them out. Would you be interested in going up there and meeting both of them?" He stood there waiting for a response. I knew the decision needed a quick reply.

"Sure," I said with a smile. "I'd like to meet them."

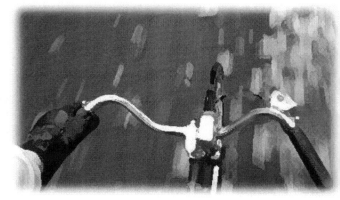

A few days passed. And with my parents' utmost approval, I traveled by bicycle over to Ridge Street to personally meet Mr. & Mrs. Wilmer. Right from the start, you could not ask for a more pleasant couple to spend a day a week doing odd work, lawn cutting, painting, and chores.

Getting on my bicycle during the summer became a religion to me. One of those places I traveled to each time was the Wilmer home, helping them to keep everything in order. They always had something that needed cleaning, shaping, or just making look good again.

Sweating and pushing yourself was expected to get things done at our own house. This was no different at the Wilmer home. I kept going back because I felt I made a difference in someone's life, while others may have pushed the chance away, I just kept returning. When you keep giving, something always comes back in a new form.

The responsibility slowly shaped me into a more responsible young person. When others were playing around, I traveled on that bicycle back to the place where opportunity had called. I gave my time, my energy, and my skill to get things done for someone who appreciated help. I shall never forget how thankful they were to see me each and every time after a rain shower or on a sunny day.

When Mr. Wilmer died, I felt that would be the end of the relationship with the Wilmer family. I never thought I would spend another ten years taking care of Mrs. Wilmer. I consider it the bicycle ride that lasted twenty years – a quiet commitment that I kept to myself, and something no one knew anything about.

On every birthday, I would always get a card from them. Inside, there would be a twenty-dollar bill. The note would say: "To our hardest worker." Not one birthday was ever forgotten in all the years I worked for the Wilmer family.

I was lucky to have such a unique friendship with a couple who had lived through everything. In a day and age where responsibility lingers and the younger generation has no interest in older folks, there was something to be said about this timeless friendship.

Those were the days

Those were the days
    I felt invincible
    I felt alive
    I felt daring
I could do almost anything
But I cannot go back
    My life is not the same
In my dreams I can
Nothing has left me
    The sun will rise again
    And I will see its beauty
Those days will return
    In another place and time.

Stronger

I am stronger
For who I am
And in everything I do
I believe in myself
No matter what happens
Nothing is in my way
My spirit will emerge
I will succeed at what I try
Even time cannot fail faith
For I am stronger.

Love may give back to me

Maybe love had escaped me
For all that I thought I knew
To every dream I have had
Love may have taken it away.

I remember a time when I was alone
Every thought fell freely from my mind
And I caught it exactly in rhyme
But love had fallen short in my life.

Now I have this chance to make it
To live the dreams once set aside
A chance to jump aboard a train
That leads to the center of my heart.

I must not be afraid of boarding
To realize my personal potential
For to grow is to love is to learn
And that is the purpose of this life.

Maybe love had escaped me
For all that I thought I knew
But there are still unknown dreams
That love may give back to me.

Original: June 28, 2004

Revised: September 18, 2011

To the Fallen Solider

To the fallen solider
We owe our life's freedom to you
Through the darkest of ages
The windfalls and successes
Through conflict and bloodshed
We should not push aside the memory
Or should we ever forget the effort
Of someone who died in vain
Protecting us, defending us
Allowing peace and harmony
To return to our daily lives.

To others who have died
Throughout all the wars
You gave us free will
To actually live your life
And follow in your footsteps
We give you honor and respect
For these blessings are beyond
The beliefs of any weak-minded soul
We shall stand tall and strong
Your dreams shall provide hope
So no solider may ever fall again.

September 18, 2011

The Poet's Chair

In a dark, cool basement chamber
There sat a brown metal stool
He spent hours writing there
Laboring his thoughts away
Engrossed in the sound of music
While sharing his wisdom and grace.

He started at the tender age of seven
With a daily journal he bought
Capturing a boy turning into a man
With small failings in his days
To new love and eager ambitions
The passion burned in his heart.

One tragic day soon came along
Cancer had taken his Uncle away
He felt the need to express this love
And composed a poem about his life
In a vision he saw by a riverbed:
Rivers, he wrote, never stop giving.

Yet he would find the power in words
The brown metal stool still calling
In the depths of long, long nights
And he would continue to write
To express emotions and feelings
The morning sun would find him weak.

Poem after poem, hour after hour
One voice, one life, one dream
Because he understood the words
Of one innocent and ordinary life
A man who never stopped believing
His passion found in the Poet's Chair.

September 19, 2011

The Final Wave Goodbye

As my father drove down the road
He waved through the frozen glass
Eyes stern, followed with a smile
Nineteen years I had been his son
And tonight would be his final goodbye.

The snow fell steadily that night
Like an angel sprinkling moon dust
As I finished the neighborhood drives
And headed back home to find warmth
But found myself dreadfully alone.

I was typing a college paper
When one call changed my life
My sister's voice was so pure and calm
Telling me to come to the hospital
Where my father had just arrived.

So I steadily drove into the night
Unknowing of the reasons why
And then the snow just stopped
Allowing the stars to break wild and free
This heaviness weighed upon my heart.

Bursting into the Emergency Doors
I saw an old man lying on a gurney
No one seemed to be helping
Naked, lifeless, alone and dead
I knew, for some reason, it was him.

At the graceful age of fifty-seven
My father died in my mother's arms
Dancing with the love of his life
As the song played its final verse
His time on Earth had come to pass.

September 20, 2011

The Road to Destiny

Halftime was all I remember
With me as their head coach
A miracle had followed us along
Through a three-game winning streak
To this final basketball game
We found ourselves face-to-face
Held together by locker room dreams.

I asked the most pivotal question:
Why do you want to win this game?
It was the only thought I could muster
One girl said to win it for a best friend
And another said to win it for the parents
Such insightful ideas were suggested
We could no longer stay in that room.

All nine children had offered
The most honest ways to win
Leaving one girl to speak her mind
She had determination in her voice
And said, "Let's win this game tonight
For all the children who came before
And had failed in living their dreams."

The whole team erupted into tears
As the looks of determination spread
You could feel the room start to melt
It was the only place I wanted to be
I knew, then, they could do anything
The locker room door opened wide
As they followed their road to destiny.

September 26, 2011

My Toughest Challenge

The toughest challenge I ever faced
That turned my shyness into grace
Happened in a tiny Office Room
A standing-room crowd gathered
Waiting upon my words of wisdom
To take technology and make it sing
I had no notes in front of me to speak
Only the heart and soul of a young man
I told them stories and shed some tears
My enthusiasm peaked upon each mistake
For they saw me learn so easily from them
As I would confidently laugh at myself
So innocent and pure I had been
I knew at that moment I found my passion
To connect with others in such a way
Had long been overdue in my life
The young invert boy had stood tall
And delivered in the final seconds
Of a long-awaited match-up
Would make any father proud
Of a son who could be so honest
And, yet, never afraid to keep learning
When all else fails in this life.

September 10, 2011

9/11's Final Meaning

The challenge has been put in motion
By someone else's deeds and actions
For today is unlike any day in history:
The unending passion to succeed
And spreading that energy forward
Gathering others in your wake
To dare them to achieve, to be proud
As any American should
To find the uniqueness in yourself
For this life of ours is so precious
One that could be over in seconds
A shocking end to an aging soul
Or just taken away for no reason
You must embrace everything sacred
From this moment in your life
And push forward, your head held high
For, yet, in the passing of this day
Another one will come again
You will eventually find understanding
9/11's deepest meaning revealed:
Live life fully, with vigor and determination
For we are all survivors and dreamers
And our lives hold more value now
Than any time in our nation's history.

September 11, 2011

Birthday Bells

Your life shall have touches of grace
Growing in a world of ordinary wisdom
Making tomorrow look more like today.

Each should be lived like anyone else's life
Celebrating them with many birthday bells
As you age through the bounds of time.

Let time not alter one part of your character
Or let any deep losses reshape your mind
For you need a clear path to find freedom.

Each year you get somewhat closer
To a richer and more meaningful life
Through the efforts of your own honest labor.

Let your spirit stay forever young and enduring
Willing to succeed at any challenge or request
As the ringing of birthday bells can be heard.

October 9, 2011

One Special Companion

I have a special companion
Sleeping next to me in a tiny, round bed
A brown-haired blue-eyed beagle boy
With enough vinegar and spunk
To last all the days through.

Every morning he is ready
To catch the new scent of the day
Or maybe find a meaty treat
Waiting in his spotted bowl
His stomach never seems full.

With all the love in his eyes
He gives me happiness and joy
In each simple walk or car ride
He faithfully gives without command
Loving looks and careful licks.

His stinky breath gives warmth
On the coldest winter's day
And his bouncy, crazy walk
Leaves others to see a trademark
That could win him a grand prize.

He is a boy that has many names
But responds to a high-pitch tone
When dinner time comes along
Or his desire to go on a hunt
Regardless it is day or night.

One day I will find his bed empty
And he shall never be forgotten
Through time he became my best friend
His spirit will live in everything
And he will be with me through and through.

September 14, 2011

Each Morning

Each morning as the sun rises
You shall find the day pull upon
The strings of your heart
Whether good nor bad
Whether right nor wrong
Lucky to find the feeling return
You are alive, well, and moving
Through the bounds of time
And nothing will get in its way.

The Drive

The first moment of a drive
Tests the reflexes of tired muscles
Challenges the looking eye
As it pulls us back in our seats
The drive takes us to the unknown
No destination in mind
No place off limits
Open your window to feel a breeze
Flowing through your hair
The open road grabs hold of you
And if you follow it long enough
Freedom shall find you.

In the Depth of a Mind

To see the world anew
In the depth of a mind
Crossing through countries
Sailing through the ages
A mind not finished yet
With life's little questions.

I am a man of integrity
To see the new light
And to draw answers
From things misunderstood
This is the task at hand
My private little gift.

The power of a mind
Starts with the meaning
Of how it achieves
And how it thrives
To design new meanings
From other gifted thinkers.

A whole lifetime
Will never reveal
The true meaning
Of my beautiful birth
And the chance I was given
To struggle to a higher ground.

September 8, 2011

A Referee's Conflict

You could see the blood-shot eyes look at me as I stood face-to-face with a person I did not know. I saw the sun beginning to set behind one of the basketball hoops, and I tried to find peace in that thought as this man continued to swear and curse. It was a hot summer day in June, and I was dressed in a black and white striped shirt, black pants, and black shoes. I was a young twenty-five-year-old referee on that court doing a tournament. But I just could not say anything to this man. I did not know him. He was just a player on a basketball team and I had just finished the last game.

As a registered basketball official, you would think there would be little conflicts in working a game. The process is simple: you drive to the tournament, referee the games, sign the score book, collect your earnings, and go home. Fans and coaches may get upset and voice an opinion, but the game usually finishes without delay. But if you have never officiated, then you would be unaware of these conflicts that go on behind the scenes.

His words could have hurt any intelligent person. He made me deal with something I had no idea how to handle.

As the story goes, the player approached me after the game and went into a tirade about how he had been cheated and taken advantage of during the day. He worked me over with his harsh words and throwing his arms up and down, trying to use intimidation to make me fight him. At one moment, it seemed the potential for violence was there. Instead, I offered him the shirt off my back, to see how I see it game in and game out, and to understand that not every drive to the basket was a foul. I wanted him to understand me, but instead he turned and walked away.

I found myself feeling worry, anger, concern, and helplessness that day. The only word that describes this incident was conflict. I was having a conflict with another person. Better yet, the player was having a conflict with my officiating style. Most of us are not well-versed in dealing with conflicts.

This conflict began as a simple disagreement in opinion over the course of an entire day. During the games he played, he wanted a call to be made and used verbal threats to get his point across. He wanted the call to be a foul against the opposing player. Since there was such little contact between the two players, there was nothing for me to call. There was nothing done about it. He had to respect my observation and refereeing style, but he continued to verbally lash out at me again and again.

We must accept the fact, then, that we will have to deal with conflicts in our life. The same applies to that basketball court on a hot summer day. There are many reasons why people become impatient, short-fused, and argumentative. For example, concerns about losing one's job to a close loved one dying have stretched our minds and patience. We are stressed out from the act of living each day. We bottle up these emotions and bring them to awkward moments in life. This player, perhaps, may have lived through something horrible that left him feeling empty inside and volatile. This would be the perfect formula to take a simple conflict and make it something larger than life.

That one summer day has not left me. I remember clearly how I was gaining my first experiences with players and fans, and spending the day alone working a court. When the incident happened, it was the last game of the day. I was tired and wore out from the day's events. I had worked twenty games, and I found myself looking face-to-face with someone who did not like me or what I stood for. He wanted a resolution now and I had nothing to offer him. I still feel I need to answer his questions, and not cheat him out of fair play.

Since that day, he left me thinking about the simplest act of listening. This is something I am still learning about to this day. I am not afraid to admit that maybe I did not listen to his issues or care for his concerns. Now I listen hard to another person's opinions or suggestions. You cannot disregard someone else because you do not agree with them; you have to open your mind and put yourself in their shoes. You have to allow yourself to experience worry, anger, concern, and even helplessness. It is a natural part of being able to grasp both sides of an issue. You also need good toleration skills to be able to keep your perspective about a given conflict. The hope is you find a plausible solution and both sides can leave satisfied.

November 5, 2009

What can I leave behind after death?

What can I leave behind after death?
A small memory of a beautiful day
Or maybe the sound of crashing waves
Moving along a distant shoreline
Or the first love in a teenager's life
A tiny bird running along the road
Or maybe a severe lightning storm
I know that nothing will ever be forgotten
Although I will take a different form
The memories shall live somewhere
Wrapped in a box with this poem
To be read someday by someone
Who shall remember just one line
That would inspire my departed heart.

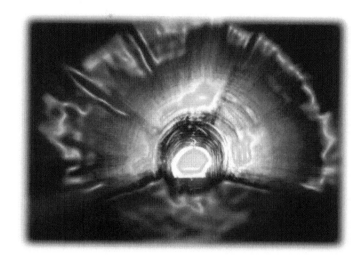

September 8, 2011

While No One Watches Me

I had always tried in my life
To be the best I could be
At everything possible
Whether it be sport or job
I tried and tried with all my effort
Not everyone is so driven
To cast a stone in the water
And watch what happens
It may have been a curious mind
That kept a child like me
Reaching for the stars
Trying to be a champion
When no one else was around
When others had closed their doors
To watch me take my victory lap
When only a neighborhood eye
Watched my special moment
How many times I have lived
A moment where I had won
A moment when I had achieved
A moment that defined me.

I had always tried in my life
To be the best I could be
And I do not think I ever failed
For it was for those who never tried
Are the ones who never stood tall
Whether by fact or fiction
Knew in their hearts they won
It was in the thought of it all
That I found the way to the gold
The very meaning is true to my heart
Like every effort it took to get there
Had been worth every ounce of sweat
And I should never look down upon
Even the smallest victories gained
That has given me the desire to do
So much more beyond myself
For it is in the giving of one's self
That I think makes the difference
Between a winner and a loser
Someone who never stops trying
While no one watches me.

I do not want to grow old

I do not want to grow old
Unable to get out of bed
To forget the day's routines
Or stumble upon the floor.

I do not want to grow old
The body aches all the time
Everything falls silent
And the light is not as bright.

I do not want to grow old
Becoming the odd duck out
The butt of every inside joke
And guided by someone else.

I do not want to grow old
But soon time will beckon my name
The choice shall not be of my own
And I will fall into my lonely self.

October 1, 2011

The Teacher

You shall profess before your students
The ideals and methods of learning
Your years of training and education
Have taken you to this moment.

You can turn a theory into reality
Before a class of eager students
Their minds are open to understand
How the world really surrounds them.

To touch one life means goodness
To touch one life is to touch the future
To touch one life creates change
To touch one life is to be a teacher.

You shall forever be a teacher
And you cannot escape the title
For you have earned its dignity
And are now bounded by its grace.

And to those that keep sharing
A passion of knowledge and lure
You can always be rest assured
Your spirit will live on through others.

October 1, 2011

Sidewalks

A wood sidewalk lies near a silent camp road
And successful travelers follow along its path
While winds penetrate its delicate surface
Many hours will pass and fold as the wood fades
From nature's own water, snow and ice
And **varnish** protects its special life.

A clay sidewalk lies near a bumpy county highway
And hardened travelers follow along its path
While winds penetrate its fragile surface
Many days will pass and fade as the clay splits
From nature's own water, snow and ice
And **endurance** shelters its unique life.

A cement sidewalk lies near a busy city street
And worldly travelers follow along its path
While winds penetrate its frail surface
Many years will pass and fade as the cement cracks
From nature's own water, snow and ice
And **judgment** defines its exceptional life.

October 1, 2011

Little Things

There is something about little things
That can truly shape your life
Take notice of smaller details
And watch for the changing light.

It takes an inquisitive eye
And the heart to make it happen
For the world is forever changing
And we need your consideration.

Like a famous puzzle maker
You organize and finally resolve
Those tiny pieces start forming
The main parts shape themselves.

There is something about little things
As your memories fade to black
You could make the difference
And help this world stay intact.

September 26, 2011

The Sound of Silence

Living in silence cannot hold back
The true meaning of a good life.

For each second of perception
Gives us so many blessings.

Although one sense is lost
The others turn stronger.

We have to breakthrough
From the sound of silence.

The potential of one grand existence
Moves us closer to a healthier world.

A world where we hear
The endless sound of drums.

Taking us away from sadness
And pushing fear aside forever.

September 30, 2011

A Miracle for Two

We had passed through the first light
And the ease of talking guided us
As my mother and I traveled home
After a late-night speaking engagement.

The car rumbled along in style
But the road was full of wetness
For a storm had just passed through
And the car felt smooth and loose.

My mother first noticed the strange vehicle
Which was moving rather leisurely
Down the hillside toward the next light
And this odd sensation crept up my spine.

The light ahead had moved into view
My car cruising at hydroplaning speed
The road seemed like a reflection of glass
As the light was now just seconds away.

The flashing yellow light glimmered
As I watched this car creep along
And then stopped in the middle of my path
Leaving me seconds to decide my life.

I remembered the laughter and the tears
The first ride with my driver's license
The sixty-five foot shot I made in a game
The first fish I caught with my father.

The brake pedal was left untouched
And death had started to open its doors
A miracle for two needed to happen
Not to let a mother and son die together.

At the moment of impact the car moved
As I swerved the car slightly to the left
Silence loomed as I missed the bumper
And we drove on, alive, into the night.

October 6, 2011

Patience

In today's world of give and take
We have failed to realize one thing:
Our patience has become a lost art
One that keeps us in harmony and sync.

A cell phone rings on our side pocket
And the need to answer is so profound
But remember to wait and slumber
You can be separated for one day.

You will find that patience can be found
In the simplest form of human action
Like riding your bicycle or taking a brisk walk
Even finding a lost road in a deep forest.

We could all use a break at times
This stress level builds in our minds
And we need to find that peacefulness
To guide us back to a fulfilling life.

It has and always will be patience
So let us not lose sight of its uniqueness
The power of a patient soul touches many
And creates a balance in a rushed world.

October 6, 2011

One Tree in the Pasture

I saw you again while driving to work
Near a farmer's hill along the county line
One tree standing alone in the pasture.

Please tell me the meaning of life
Of how the world is held together
By tiny strands of thick, aged bark.

Many have passed you by each day
Without ever noticing your shadows
Or the strength it takes to stand tall.

I have often wondered how it could be
You have ended up alone and abandoned
Never sharing your life with anyone.

You exemplify everything noble and enduring
With a simple wave of a leaf or branch
You give this world a wealth of your faith.

You have lived through many seasons
Winds shaking and pulling at your roots
The lack of water withering your branches.

You have grown beyond the golden years
The glow of the setting sun will soon fall
And I pray you will see just one more day.

October 7, 2011

The Hardest Game of My Life

While crossing Michigan's famous Mackinac Bridge, I had known from the start I was going into a world I had never seen before. The miles sailed along, tree by tree, as I traveled further south on I-75, heading towards a big July weekend basketball tournament at Central Michigan University. I had a chance to see the sun set over the side view mirror as I traveled into the night to my destination.

A good friend of mine, Gene Schuett, had hired me to referee the Red Hacker, a traveling basketball tournament with plenty of piss and vinegar for all ages to witness. The Red Hacker had a history of people going off the deep-end at these tournaments. They wanted to make sure they got their $80 dollars' worth.

The day was a difficult adventure in endurance. You had to officiate a court all by yourself, score the games by yourself, and deal with frustrated players by yourself. You had to also keep the game time, which ran twenty minutes for a 4-on-4 game and up to sixteen points to declare the winner. The hardest job, above all this busyness, was to keep the games going on-time, regardless of the various outcomes one could imagine in basketball. I had worked other Red Hacker tournaments in Sault Ste. Marie and Petoskey over the past two years, so I knew that being on-time was a plus.

The game time can become your nightmare if it is not kept correctly. I had seen for myself other courts where they were still working at 7 pm, about two hours over the required time allotment. That makes for a long day when you have to be on your feet for a twelve-hour period, with hardly any rest time and loud rap music blaring in your ears all day. The beat of the music eventually deafens out the shouting from "sideline referees" who are working you over game-by-game to get a foul called or to just reveal offensive gestures as you run by them.

Mr. Schuett had planned out where he was going to place me for the tournament: a top-ranked court with all black players, and me being the only white guy. When I got the assignment, I knew that my hands were going to be full with attitudes and harsh looks from people I did not know or even want to know. I also knew the skill level would be at a high level, for the players were adults in their twenties.

It seemed like a perfect recipe for an eminent disaster.

The first game started at 8 am with little disruption. I sensed that many of the players were fresh out of bed, missing shots left and right, and not playing any defense on both ends of the court as the scoring went wild. My calls were quick and sudden; I put players at the line; I called fouls in a fair manner. I do not remember anyone in particular giving me a hard time or causing a distraction in gameplay. The day seemed peaceful and in order, and I was anxious to finish the morning games on-time and ahead of schedule, just like the games I had worked in Petoskey.

The 8:30 am game had a different flavor and intensity, starting from the moment the "rock and scissor" battle determined possession. I could see these two teams had faced each other before in other tournaments. Familiar grins and hand-shaking gestures happened in a pleasant and respectful manner. From what I could gather, this was going to be the toughest game of the day.

The intense match-up lived up to its reputation. We had full-court pressing, fast-break dunks, incredible dribbling skills, beautiful breakaways, yelling and screaming at one another on defense, and girlfriends who really loved their boyfriends all out hustle and sweat for a three pointer. The entertainment value had reached its peak when the score was at 15-14 with one minute left in the game.

That was when everything changed from competition to all-out war.

The play that changed everything was an apparent shoving match between two players in the right corner of the court. The moment happened so fast I had no way of sliding my body in between the players to stop the apparent fist-throwing motions. As the one player swung forward with this fist, the other player ducked, landing a punch into the face of a young boy who stood along the sidelines. The punch caused the boy to fall towards the ground in a hard manner, blood pouring from the side of his face.

The son's mother jumped right up and pointed at my face. "You better do something about this. My son is hurt. Do you hear me? Do you hear me?"

I responded, "Yes, ma'am. I will get these men to come over and apologize to your son. I will take care of it."

The apology part seemed over the top to me. I did not know what to do, and Gene was not around to give me instruction. I gathered the basketball and decided it best to leave the court to gather my thoughts about how I would handle this mess.

An old lady stood at the other corner of the court, blocking my path to exit the commotion and confusion of the moment. She piped up and said, "Where do you think you are going? You can't leave this court. You can't go anywhere."

I looked her dead-eye in the face and said, "I can go where I want. I'm the referee. But I will be back. You keep an eye on things." And I walked right past the cranky old lady.

Running away from this issue was not the solution. I wanted to just leave the gymnasium, get in my car, watch the trees flow past my window, and drive the 600 miles home to forget this ever happened. No Gene in sight. I had no options but to get some water and sit at a table upstairs away from the commotion. I knew everyone would be waiting for my return, for basketball players never leave an unfinished game.

I remember sitting alone at the table for about twenty minutes, and no ideas had come to mind. I knew my options were running out.

But another official sat down next to me. He said, "How is your day going?"

"I have a bad one going at my court. One of the players hit a child in the face by accident. I don't know what to do," I said with concern. "The players are waiting for me. Gene is nowhere to be found."

He said, strangely enough, "Just go and take care of business. You are the man of that court. You own it! You rule it! Just take care of business." He stood up, holding a water bottle in his hand and smiled. "They don't know you have the power. They have no idea what that is. Show them."

And the stranger got up and walked back down the hallway.

The blood flowed in my veins and my thoughts focused on a final decision. I got up with purpose and a plan to get myself through the hardest moment of my life. My thoughts kept drifting back to a time when I felt invincible, I felt alive, and I felt daring enough to face any task with determination. Whatever fear I had been feeling just melted away.

Upon my return to the court, the old lady looked at me with a snarly grin and said, "Back for some more, kid. We missed you."

I looked her dead-eye in the face and said, "I think it's time to get this show on the road. Pardon me, lady." She snarled at me one last time as I passed her by.

The two players who had started the fight were now facing each other in a conference with me. I first asked each player to explain what happened in detail. Of course, each story was one that had blamed the other for punching the kid. Neither player would take responsibility for their action, leaving me at a moment where I was going to forfeit the game.

I made sure I said it out loud to both teams – "If neither of you apologize to the boy, I will forfeit this game right now. You have to tell me what your decision is going to be."

There was commotion and arguing going on around me, with swearing and yelling to get them to do the right thing. Both teams worked their players over, and after several minutes, these two players approached me and said they would apologize.

They approached the boy and both said, "I'm very sorry." The son's mother was so proud that she hugged me on the spot.

"Thank you. My son loves basketball. You said you would get them to apologize. I'm so happy you did this." Her smile seemed like it would never leave her face. She could never be more proud of her son, blood and all, than from that second on.

I turned toward both players and proclaimed, "You are both ejected."

"What the hell? You can't eject me," the one player screamed.

I looked them both in the face and said, "Look, under the rules of this tournament, any fighting means an automatic ejection. Even in high school basketball, the ruling is the same. You are both ejected. Let's finish the game right now! I will not wait. The ball is in play right here!" I pointed to the baseline and stood there waiting with the ball.

The two players walked off the court and to the sideline. They were very upset, but I was showing power and control. Both players had no idea this was coming, and I think I leveled them with this comment.

"I will call the game off. The ball is right here!" I pointed again to the spot.

The ball was put into play by the team who was ahead. This long pass was thrown to the other end of the gym, caught in the hands of the tallest guy on the court, and slammed-dunked into the net for the win. Beautiful play! Final score: 16-14.

Do you think anyone approached me? Was I harassed by fans or by parents? Do you think anyone complained about the final moments? Did anyone say anything? Not one thing happened. I stood by myself at center court and waited for the next game to start. The day would be peaceful again, and I knew that everything would be all right.

In the end, this one game took a total of one hour to finish, but only ten seconds to conclude the final play of the game. I had two ejections and one tough decision to make. It was, by far, the hardest game of my life.

September 2, 2011

Lake Superior

Lake Superior will always amaze me
My ever-lasting friend and mentor
The true inspiration of nature's glory
A constant reminder of beauty and power
It seems you run off the face of the Earth
And your deepest blue can be seen for miles.

Spring carries these enduring moments:
The snow melts
The birds sing
The flowers grow
The grass sprouts
And you warm and sparkle in the sunshine.

I have traveled your shoreline for years
Listening to the constant sound of waves
Moving sand and placing it all around
To create breath-taking beaches
The most amazing sunrises and sunsets
Year after year you never fail to deliver.

You are never shy to hold back secrets
Of how you will live beyond the generations
Showing your heart to millions of others
Never stopping to take a break from work
Always going the extra mile to boldly impress
Another traveler who comes to your water's edge.

October 7, 2011

The Old Farmhouse

Standing near the base of the hill
One can still see the old farmhouse
Its torn roof and dried wood planks
Blends with the surrounding pasture
The golden sun shines every day
For wonderful memories of this place
Are bursting out in subtle moments
Silence dominates the landscape
And the only activity is the wind
Colliding with the morning air
While the heavy dew blows away.

You can still find this old farmhouse
Near a small American country road
Yet these buildings are left alone to die
But the spirits of those who lived there
Will never leave such a blessed place
And the seasons will come again
The years will fade into distant memory
Allowing this one vision to be left
Of an old farmhouse and hillside
Waiting for life and liberty to return
And breathe life back into an old friend.

October 8, 2011

The Road Taken

He talked about roads and choices
And he saw this in nature's imagery
Knowing how this challenged minds.

Resting inside thousands of wallets
His words are waiting to be recited again
By someone who needs his guidance.

Life means something more now
As we take a good look at ourselves
And learn a new meaning each time.

Remember one hundred years ago
A young man walked into his own pasture
And saw two roads diverged in a yellow wood.

The vision happened upon one glorious day
As he considered life's endless possibilities
And his decision lives on in those who follow it.

October 8, 2011

The Passing Train

My tiny little room sits silent and still
As I await the arrival of a timely train
The clock seems to be frozen
I hear the sound of a whistle blowing
As the passing train draws near.

At once the room shakes and rattles
An old poetry book falls against another
Pencils roll around a small table
A golden necklace dangles freely in the air
And a stuffed animal drops to the floor.

I know the peak of the passing
As the loud clinking rail expresses
The value of its cargo being pulled
Eventually finding other towns and cities
Making its way home somewhere in America.

We all can connect to the passing train
It showcases America's strength and integrity
A simple gateway to an industrious past
A reminder of those who moved our country
And delivered much needed goods, day or night.

October 9, 2011

Money. You earn, spend, and save it. Billions of printed pieces of paper float from city to city, wallet to wallet, and from country to country. Without money, you would not have a roof over your head, a car to travel in, a bed to rest upon, or a good meal in your belly. One simple little transaction has transformed a world with forms of goodness, pain, death, diversity, and greed.

You wonder how much more different our lives would be if we had a chance to win a million dollars. Would our days become easier? Could we live the rest of our lives without working as hard? Or would everyone want something from us? The chances are that life would be just as intense and difficult even if we did not have the money in the first place. Just think: one second you have nothing; the next moment you have everything.

Long ago, our family came close to winning one million dollars.

My father played the lottery for over twenty years. When my father passed away when I was 19, he left behind a black booklet at his workplace. Inside the booklet were pages and pages of lottery numbers, written by hand, week after week, for a twenty-year period. He had played every week in the black booklet. His picks were written next to the winning ones. The booklet's tattered cover told the tale of someone who had spent many hours writing numbers, thinking about the possibilities, and dreaming about cracking the code to become the next big winner.

And he had kept this secret from our family for all those years.

One Saturday night when I was seventeen years old, my father gave me a lottery ticket he had purchased for the 7:30 pm drawing. He told me to see if the numbers matched (while he continued to watch the hockey game in the other room).

It was the first time I had ever watched the television show.

After a brief commercial, I remember the first white numbered ball rolling down and toward the television screen: 16. I glanced back at the ticket: 16. A few seconds later, another ball rolled down: 28. I glanced to the ticket again: 28. The perspiration started to roll down my face and I had felt my stomach churn some as I realized the matches in my hand. I quietly stared at the screen as the remaining numbers, one by one, came rolling into my steady eyes. Each number that matched made me want the next one to match even more – and I got my wish as each one did! And then the final number came upon the screen, and my heart froze and this joy erupted. I jumped up and down, telling my mother, "Mom, the numbers match, the numbers all match."

My sister had entered through the front door and saw all the commotion. She had no idea that we had just won a million dollars. "Wendy," I yelled, "we just won the lottery." She hugged my mother and we were all jumping up and down with joy, tears flowing upon our faces. It seemed like nothing was in our way to announce the good news to my father.

We all sprinted into that back bedroom. My father was still sitting there watching a hockey game and smoking a cigarette.

"Dad, the ticket is a winner; the numbers all match. You won a million dollars," as I pointed to the ticket with pride. I handed him the ticket and he took a quick look at the date.

"Oh, that's last week's ticket. I gave you the wrong one," he sternly said. Then he was back to watching the game.

This chill ran through my body and down to my feet. I just stood there and could say nothing to him. Our once smiling faces had turned sad and we all left the room without a sound. I felt deflated and empty with regret that the ticket was the wrong one. I just couldn't believe he had no reaction at all, not even an ounce of concern in his voice. He acted like nothing had happened that day.

Maybe my father knew that one day would never come true. He liked his job working on trains at the railroad station, the relationships he had with his co-workers, and even the habit of driving up the county road to go there five days a week. He had a lot at stake if he were to win. I think he had mentally prepared himself to never win and solve the puzzle.

The money, however, could have helped out our family in so many ways. From the clearing of life debts to the places and opportunities that were always out of our reach, the money could have given us a chance to live easier, to live a richer and fuller life.

Money. I am glad we did not win it. I could easily give you a million reasons why. As I have grown older, I am happy to say I have worked hard for everything I have ever owned, have taken great pride in each accomplishment I have ever made, and I am always telling others to find something they care deeply about and to live out their dreams. A million dollars would not have developed me into this person who believes in so much. You could not put a dollar amount on something that you are passionate about. My father may have saved me from falling into that line of thinking that money means everything.

His little black booklet challenged my own life and it lives on through me. I am the million dollar winner.

My Saving Grace

It happened on a cold winter's day
As I hopped along the campus path
To find myself opening a heavy door
To the West Science Building lab.

One week before I was walking fine
But I had been injured in a pickup game
And I could no longer stand straight
Without the aid of a long pair of crutches.

The clock had shown five minutes to ten
As I hurried along to find the staircase
For I was not considered a needy candidate
To receive the ever-golden elevator pass.

I started the tedious task of hopping
Balancing myself with a backpack aboard
I envisioned reaching the very top step
And going to class like many times before.

But then my one support slipped away
And I felt my body falling backwards
Aimlessly drifting in the morning cool air
And I had no time to react to the fright.

This hand jammed up against my back
A young man had come from behind
My saving grace never said any words
He bowed his head and went on his way.

An angel had been watching over me
And I wish I could tell him something more
Thankful words and praises are not enough
To let him know his effort changed one life.

October 9, 2011

My Closing Words

The day is soon in closing
And the light will soon blow out.

To this day I have given my all
And there is nothing more to say.

But does the day really end?
Or is something about to begin?

Darkness sees its chance
And puts our hearts at rest.

It seems a lifetime has passed
In this small moment of time.

The Judgment Day has arrived
To let go of struggles and pains.

To live and have lived
And to find peace again.

Life seems so bright
When the sun returns.

As I slowly close my tired eyes:
These words now live forever.

September 12, 2011

The Road of Life

There are many travelers on the road of life
Passing others by without even noticing
Moving in the flow of a demanding lifestyle
In the quickest and most efficient manner.

You may begin to wonder what they gain
Their edginess shows to every observer
As they pass with such risky maneuvers
A life of hasty judgment and little reasoning.

The speedometer sits steady around fifty-five
As you see an old abandoned farmhouse
Observe two trees standing near a meadow grove
And watch the sun set at the end of a summer's day.

All of life can be witnessed through a car window
On a daily commute into town each morning
And you would be surprised the innocence you find
The day can unfold in such beautiful ways.

The speed of life can never be measured
By how fast or slow it takes to get somewhere
It is about noticing little things along the ride
That really begin to shape the road of life.

October 15, 2011

The Fear of Technology

Technology now flows in our bloodstream
As corporations create more and more
Teasing us with a fancy gadget that does it all
Discovering thousands of informational sources
From either a laptop or a tiny smartphone.

Our human existence has slowly disappeared
Over the past twenty years of technology use
For some part of our dignity is dying
As our youth fail to see the real picture.

With screen-image words appearing
Not that of human emotions and efforts
Or even by small talk or a simple handshake
We have become a generation lacking dreams.

The fear grows to our future children
Who lack the skills and beliefs to express
To make solid decisions under pressure
And to have a complete desire to be a survivor.

Our world never saw this one coming
The dreams of gifted engineers celebrated
In their private meetings and well-paid jobs
As they step forward and we step back.

We have chances to improve the bitter void
And to find the balance between man and machine
Not to become a robot and live in silence
We must let passion save us from technology.

October 11, 2011

Marquette, Michigan

The glory of a beautiful northern town
Enchants every visitor who comes here
You will find people who work hard and play
And are just minutes from nature's calling
Nestled hours away from anything else
A real find to those who drive this way
A life so pleasant, fair, kind, and free
This can only be Marquette, Michigan.

From the largest wooden dome in the world
To a special island visited by thousands
A lakeshore boulevard ride that never ends
To the biggest fresh water lake known to man
A large mountain side reached by foot
The rich variety of Washington Street shops
And the beauty of everything never lets you forget
You are closer to Heaven here than anywhere.

To those who have left are always bound to return
One cannot forget the "**living**" that takes place
As each season arrives and departs with visions
A place that inspires the artists and dreamers
To take just one more look across the landscape
You might see an eagle fly and find its waiting nest
Many have stayed to live out their remaining days
To take a final breath of Marquette's freshest air.

October 12, 2011

First Frisbee Throw

We have all wanted to throw a Frisbee
To display our determination and manly strength
Watching the thing fly so high into the sky
Like it were never to return to Mother Earth
A toy that fulfilled many childhood dreams.

Behind that throwing arm was a good child
A relentless, curious mind to try anything
Even throwing one from the back hill ledge
While a father watched from down below
Waving through a back door window sill.

The boy stood there with all his dreams aside
As he happily waved and let this Frisbee fly
Trying to put the thing up and over the house
And to safely land upon the neighborhood road
But the act of mother nature had other plans.

The sharp wind took and brought it down
In a quick, evasive manner he never knew
His first Frisbee throw went toward the back door
The sound of breaking glass filled the night-time air
As his father's hand beckoned him slowly inside.

October 12, 2011

One Piano Melody

There are not enough words
That truly inspire someone to believe
Only in the form of a piano melody
Played so sweetly and precise
Can open minds surely gone astray.

These notes carry into our soul
Finding a way to lift our hearts
But one melody boldly comes back
And finally releases the inner beauty
Of another world waiting to be heard.

The day may have passed away
The year galloping into the unknown
The memories fading into nothingness
The falling tear dried to the touch
But this melody never fails in giving.

That, honestly, is enough to inspire
Even the most ordinary man alive
True innocence flowing from within
Finding its way to a waiting ear
When words are just not enough.

October 13, 2011

One Chance

You may feel you do not need a church
Or someone in life to preach you the word
Like an angel has protected you from harm's way
Finding everlasting peace and harmony
Away from the present evil that lurks nearby.

Your face may never be blessed by holy water
A soul failing to reach the Sunday church
Sharing with others in the discovery of God
That many worship and treasure with eternal love
Knowing that one life had been sacrificed for all.

A stranger may come your way before long
Telling you the world will be ending too soon
And to prepare yourself to be lifted to the heavens
And to understand what this calling may mean
While others will be left behind asking why.

But you have been given just one chance
To unlock the closed mind of an aging man
Allowing God's grace to swirl in your heart
Answering all questions about life's mysteries
Following others towards the Gates of Heaven.

October 13, 2011

Cross upon the hill

You shall remember me in your dreams
As my life will soon come to pass
Remembered only by these words
Fresh rain will scatter this land.

The fresh rain will soon turn to snow
Until night falls and brings to light
How profoundly you miss me
Wild winds will shake this land.

Will you be able to join in the celebration
Of a life lived fully in every imaginable way
Trumpet melodies fill the empty pasture side
The bright yellow sun covers this land.

I will forever be living inside your thoughts
As I rest above the cross upon the hill
Where I will keep a watchful, curious eye
New seasons will transform this land.

October 13, 2011

Life through a window sill

Winter's imagery can be seen each year
In priceless pictures and in endless moments
Providing visions to a waiting audience.

Like the snow-covered branch of a birch tree
Or rubber tire tracks stitched into the snow
And the slipping and sliding neighborhood friend.

And they just keep coming day-by-day
The coldest days are not always the toughest
So much of life takes place through a window sill.

Like baby grass stems buried in a foot of snow
Or massive plows that clear dead end country roads
And old local newspapers lost in deep snow banks.

We must learn to celebrate each and every season
No matter how cold, dreadful, and disappointing
They are living, artistic visions of a changing world.

Like groups of children dragging their sleds
Or fresh snow covering city sidewalks
And black dirt mixed with mounds of white snow.

In the end we really begin to appreciate
That seasons connect with our own way of living
Guiding a soul to a lifetime of peace and harmony.

October 14, 2011

Telling the Truth

Telling the truth is really an easy thing
To tell someone what really matters
And not to hide beyond yourself
You have feelings and emotions
Riding on every word you say
These ideas can shape and mold
As you grow older and wiser.

It is not a good thing to be in a lie
For you begin to doubt the truth
For truth never has any lie to hold
You have to swallow your nervousness
Begin to understand that opening up
Is a huge part of being human and alive
Mistakes and failures build your character.

So your moment has come to let go
And finally speak the honest truth
You will feel better knowing you did right
By not letting the fear hold back
Someone will appreciate you more
For clearing the air to another who cares
Will all come back to you later in life.

October 11, 2011

Distant Cloud

A whisper of calm air has carried you here
Traveling over sundry areas of land and sea
As you chase the sun until the end of time.

We wonder where your journey had begun
Maybe around the world for business or pleasure
Meeting up with friends – no one really knows!

The heavenly sky shows us one distant cloud
It has seen rain, snow, sunshine all day through
And upon each return you brighten many hearts.

The mystery still surrounds your existence
Shared with thousands of other drifting clouds
As you try to find a place in a lonely world.

The minutes turn to hours as you float away
Today you have reached the sky's outer edge
And we wonder if you will ever come back.

A frightening end awaits you months from now
As rough winds and time will tear you a part
But your spirit lives on and shall never leave us.

October 15, 2011

Mountain Valley High

Each spring I had this one goal
To climb up Mountain Valley High
A hike just one mile from my home.

You can scale up a steep grade
Slippery rocks all around your feet
And slowly work your way to the top.

A secret little mountain view side
Nestled between homes and old roads
The city lights glow until morning breaks.

The mountain always keeps whistling
No matter how long I have been away
The massive rock wants to be your friend.

The years are aging my watchful eye
And I am not close anymore to the mountain side
But deep within a small part yearns to climb.

Maybe it is the sheer challenge and the sweat
To find yourself, again, topping the highest peak
Still leaves me restless each and every night.

October 15, 2011

America's Highways

There is nothing like the feeling of a highway
With its twists and turns into the deep unknown
You can travel it for a lifetime and never finish
The next unforeseen corner is what pulls you in
It could be a huge hillside ride to the very bottom.

One minute you are within the city limits
The next you are near a lakeside beach
The ride pushes your imagination to the end
The longer you drive; the more intense
As the world keeps changing around you.

The urge to stop and take it all in now waits
The power of the road keeps you inside
Should you rest for a while or power on through
For this long journey has no final destination
As your eyes reflect the white lines of a highway.

Now thousands of miles behind the wheel
The worn tires rolling across the rough surface
Hour-by-hour you follow down your dream
A road that bends and twists like a rocking chair
And then it straightens out for fifty-five more.

America's highways are patiently waiting for us
Put your car into drive and heed to the calling
From city to countryside you see life's pictures
Of the lives of millions of people endlessly moving
The heartbeat of the road exists in the miles that pass.

October 16, 2011

Journey into Autumn

The sign read "Journey into Autumn"
As leaves were gently falling nearby
We feel another season has come upon us
While animals hurry along digging and hauling
And strong winds whip and churn trees.

This is nature's chance to splendor and shine
Just one more color display for all the world
And then stay alone, cold, and barren
Through many blustery Winter nights to live
Soon new buds will reach for warm light.

The imagery will soon fade to autumn
You wish it were able to stay all-year long
Coloring the forest with reds and yellows
Miles and miles of bold green and gold
So many to count, so little time to share.

We take with us the power of its color
A reminder that trees are never forgotten
For they provide constant shelter and warmth
No matter what nature may throw at us
They leave behind a deep, lasting impression.

October 17, 2011

Rainbows and Dreams

One day the bright colors fell from the sky
A rainbow had come after a brief rain
Filling the skyline with its vivid color and hope
Leaving a pot of gold far in the distance
And a new beginning seemed to be at hand.

It appeared that rainbows and dreams
Had joined together for all the world to see
And anyone could climb aboard those arches
Fulfilling anything your mind could imagine
To never return to the life you once knew.

It has been said that rainbows have no ends
That they last for a brief moment and disappear
But just remember when you look into the sky
That they shall return even brighter and grander
And cast their spell upon your ever-waiting eyes.

For when the heavens open their arms to you
We must not hesitate to realize the beauty
That everything has reason and purpose
A life full of its own rainbows and dreams
Just sitting there in front of us for the taking.

October 19, 2011

The Ordinary Life

The ordinary life is pulling away from our grasp
A pastime forgotten by the next generation
Passed up by a flood of technology advances
Followed by a less personal way to interact
Our human integrity slowly has drifted aside.

The ordinary life had such simple principles
Beliefs you connected with and easily conveyed
Values that brought goodness and love to everyone
Friends who shared in happiness and sorrow
A life that respected religion and believed in God.

We are now dominated by separation anxiety
Sitting alone in a room, hall, meadow, or street
Using devices to relate feelings and emotions
For we believed this would bring us closer together
Has, in reality, driven us further apart than ever before.

A small part of today's culture still grips with the loss
For they realize how our world was first shaped
The amount of effort it took to be a giver, not a taker
Finding that each day is a brand-new chance
To take back the meaning of how to live an ordinary life.

October 21, 2011

A Real Winner

I watched this team play a game last night
And they had yet to score a single point
The basketball net did not seem big enough
As the children's skills were put to the test.

My own playing days came into my waking mind
Three seasons of losing against every opponent
A dreadful memory that can never leave you alone
You would have done anything to be a real winner.

This seventh grade team had the big shot fall
And a tremendous sense of relief filled the room
As the spectators cheered wildly for just one more
To see if something magical would happen.

I wanted them to come back and win it all
Attacking, unforgiving, relentless, focused
To take the opponent's smirk off their faces
And give them the taste of a loss so deep.

It comes naturally to want another to achieve
To turn the corner and accomplish the impossible
If you could only give them the sacred knowledge
There would have been no dry eye left in the gym.

The beauty of winning comes from your heart
An act of determination in the face of uncertainty
Played out, moment by moment, for all to see
As the closing seconds run off the ticking clock.

October 21, 2011

Blessed Earth

Earth is such a blessed, sacred place
From oceans, meadows, and seashores
I have seen only a small portion of you
Learning to find the beauty in everything.

I want to set foot in every foreign land
Let my hands touch the sand and dirt
Something so rich, pure, and moving
That launches my heart into emotions.

I have always felt the Earth's guiding winds
Allowing me the ability to carry right along
Sailing in a heavenly flight to somewhere
And now I see all the visions found in books.

Our Earth has given us so many blessings
May time allow us the opportunity to live
Long enough to watch another season pass
Of a world that deeply and truly inspires.

I have only so much time to see everything
To take all the imagery, memories, and dreams
To another time and place far from this world
An afterlife full of today's visions of this Earth.

October 22, 2011

Our Journey

We stand near the center of the universe
A tiny speck of dust surrounded by stars
Our galaxy is calling us back, day-by-day
For this brief visit is just one stop of many.

The stars radiant, gentle voice can be heard
And others are leaving this world right now
Floating amidst the stars and the heavens
Only to return, someday, in the form of another.

Do not be scared to face the unknown
Or the enormous powers of our galaxy
We are all children of this vast universe
And our beginnings are locked in time.

For hundreds of years science has tried
To unlock life's endless questions of mystery
The key reasons to how this world came about
Only to fall back and let the universe go free.

We shall forever travel and visit strange places
For fate has plotted out our never-ending journey
Our memories, dreams, and feelings go with us
As we go deeper and deeper into the hands of time.

October 22, 2011

Sudden Lake

I was taking the family for a drive
In the middle of the autumn season
As we ventured across Highway 16.

Upper Michigan roads can blend together
Amid the tall and lanky wooded landscape
And in time all roads seem to look alike.

A beaded old sign stood near an empty hill
An unlikely place to see anything at all
But it lead to the mysterious Sudden Lake.

A barren dirt road led into the woods
As we crept through each waiting corner
But a more surprising vision came that day.

A lake nestled in a quiet forest reserve
The image looked like the early 1800s
A new land that had yet to be discovered.

I deeply breathed in the chilly afternoon air
And I felt a sudden warm feeling arise in me
The lake pulled me in with its steadfast beauty.

I imagined walking across that clear blue water
Surrendering myself to the spirit living there
No matter how long the journey would take.

The blue sky and gleaming lake stood still
As we backed the car out and drove away
And I knew this spirit would wait for another.

October 22, 2011

I have never stopped

I have never stopped loving you
These feelings that burn inside
As my heart races toward yours
Many times you sang this verse
A melody so sweet and pure
In the middle of the aging night.

Keep singing to me.

Heartfelt images can never withdraw
All the love in the world I have for you
I shall love you until I cannot
With every ounce of me living for you
I believe in you, as you do for me
And this shall never end, my love.

I will be with you.

Your spirit shall be in motion
You are traveling to me now
Your eyes glaze upon the road
Searching for me in your heart
Please do not give up on me yet
I have never stopped loving you.

October 23, 2011

One Haunting Voice

His haunting voice can be heard on the radio today
A young man seemly a generation ahead of time
Trapped in a world of alcohol, drugs, and rock 'n' roll
Yet prominent with his poetic thinking mind.

It has been some forty years since his passing
But the world hungers to hear his voice sing
From a growling verse in a well-played song
Or maybe a poem he wrote about strange things.

The time we had with him was incredibly brief
He gave us a vision of how our world looks to him
He broke us through to the other side of life
And he regretfully wrote his own saddening end.

Jim Morrison arouses minds with his resounding voice
As if his youthful spirit has been alive all along
While hidden away from society writing his poetry
Making a real life, a life he desperately wants to find.

Heartfelt innocence still pours from his timely songs
A voice yelling in the darkness and finding the light
Whether the world really believes he had talent
His spirit continues to connect with new hearts.

July 3, 2011

Last Day on Earth

Water will soon flow over their banks
The storms will begin and never stop
A tidal wave will cover every land mass
And leave us to drown in a watery grave.

We can prepare and pray all we want
The Gods in the heavens do not care
For our blood will spill if we survive
As we near the end of time and space.

There was an inkling from the very start
Shouting opinions heard from silent souls
The world is going to end, end too soon
We should lie ourselves down and surrender.

The cleansing of the Earth is an ancient cycle
An asteroid hitting ground and utter destruction
Our survival skills awaken from elder beliefs
And only a few shall live through the fallout.

When the water has resided back to the ocean
The land will be lifeless, empty, and flat again
But in a bitter landscape a small flower shall bloom
Nature's beauty lives on after our last day on Earth.

October 23, 2011

Fear

I am afraid to fall asleep and never wake up
I am scared of a car swerving into my lane
Fearful the bitter cold will freeze my body to death
As I free-fall one night off the world's tallest bridge.

There are things that could scare me even more
I am not willing to let a deathly voice change me
I have been lucky to have lived as long as I did
And able to turn my life's will into a meaningful one.

Your life is a vivid play among other living souls
You need to express and live each waking moment
To avoid feeling the terror of a life's deadly fate
Your heart will go on living, whether alive or dead.

The winds will blow and find you where you hide
Do not deny the wonderful spirit that stirs and lives in you
Your inner self shall always lead you down the right path
For fear can never live long enough to become a myth.

October 23, 2011

Time

Time keeps the pace and never fails to adapt
From hours to minutes to seconds to beyond.

We are no closer to the future than centuries before
For time continues along an ancestral ancient path.

Close your eyes and imagine if time stopped.

Anything created by natural forces would halt
The rivers and lakes would dry up and turn to dust.

Seasons surrender and nothing would ever grow
You would age into infinity, forever and ever.

One part of the world would shine all year long
The other part would live in a chilly, strange silence.

We realize at some point how little time we have
The clock continues to tick on the bedroom wall.

Somewhere greatness is going to prevail right now
And then a moment later something evil happens.

Open your eyes and see if anything changed.

The room you are sitting in may be the same
And the temperature still warm and inviting.

Time, however, has taken away those moments
For there are only so many left in an innocent, beautiful life.

October 25, 2011

Childhood Memories

We all remember certain memories from childhood
That sparks a feeling in the depth of our hearts
The ruggedness of growing up and living young
The mind not sharp with the ways of enduring
In a world where effort equals mounds of gold.

As a child we had so many ideals to conquer
Not only to impress parents, friends, and loved ones
But to show the world how much good we could do
Learning and growing were always expected of us
And we followed the strength and spirit of our youth.

For some of us have never left our childhood years
With boundless amounts of energy to expel anytime
Visions of creativity spilling out of the mind and body
A long run to a faraway distance can be achieved
As we are certain to show others a bounce in our step.

It has been said at the end of life we return to childhood
When time has drained us of youthful skin and energy
Our childhood memories begin to replay the moments
A place where you could play and use imagination
To create and be anything your true heart desires.

October 28, 2011

The Memory of Trees

Over the tallest hillside meadow you can see them
Near a long and winding road near a countryside
Nestled along city streets and park bench seats
A vast world surrounded by the memory of trees.

They encompass millions of images covering this land
Having survived mother nature's hardship and destruction
They reflect the way our world looked in the distant past
And they are a symbol of a peacefulness existing on Earth.

If only they could speak in tongues and tones to us
Explaining the life and ways of the generations before
We would have so much to learn from their viewpoint
For they are the only real survivors of this aging world.

Walk out any door and they will embrace your vision
A strong breeze will come and their voice can be heard
Swaying the tree back and forth in the helpless wind
And a whole lifetime of thoughts shall flow to your mind.

October 28, 2011

One Magical Jack

There are few people on this whole Earth
Who have had such enormous success
With one vivid smile and a distinct laugh
It can only be the magic and wonder of Jack.

He has portrayed many characters on film
Neurotic ones that have scared us to death
Others that have left us thinking more about life
Many roles will live beyond his living years.

He has gained so much fame and fortune
But has yet to forget his small beginnings
Growing up in a small New Jersey town
Even then he was a clown and a skilled actor.

We come back to see his movies again and again
For he seems to be bigger than the films themselves
He is the **reflection** of the common American man
And we love him for connecting us with our own flaws.

Humor seems to be Jack's personal trademark
But you can cast him in any other ordinary part
And he portrays a breath-taking role of a character's fate
His life gives us the innocence and faith to do anything.

Jack shall still be talked about twenty years from now
In small towns and cities across this entire globe
Awakening the hearts and souls of countless millions
And he will live forever on the golden matinee screen.

October 28, 2011

Each New Day

There are signs of life as the morning dew rises
Awakening the birds and the dawn of a new day
Wild animals open tired eyes to the bright sun
While a small leaf falls to the damp forest floor.

The power of a new day is starting over again
A chance to begin anew with a fresh, focused start
Any worries or concerns are yesterday's losses
The new excitement allows us to take more risks.

The day shall progress forward on its own terms
No one can predict how the day really unfolds
We live each moment with spirit and determination
And give back to a world full of endless possibilities.

Every day will start in the same mood and manner
A huge guiding star rising up from the arms of Heaven
A special shadow spreads over the entire countryside
Far-away angels and spirits protect us each new day.

October 29, 2011

The Last High School Game

The final three minutes of my last game
Cannot be found in any highlight reel
Or scribbled down in any dusty scorebook
It is like I never played a single minute.

Five of us watched the game slowly unfold
Waiting all the while for our one chance
The final basketball game of high school
Played on a cool and brisk March night.

I said to the others before we entered
"Let's play like we never played before"
As the horn blew and we entered the game
We ran on that floor chasing one dream.

I remembered the countless scrimmages
The late-night jogs on hot summer nights
Years of pushing myself harder to achieve
And tonight was the time to let that all go.

The pace changed at eighteen points down
They never passed the half-court line once
As steals, turnovers, and fouls mounted
And we had whittled it all down to six points.

The dream of winning this one drew near
As I reached to poke the ball free and score
Just one more play would bring us back
We could finally put to rest that we belonged.

I heard the loud noise of the gym horn blow
As I looked over to see five starters standing by
I never imagined being pulled out of that game
Until I sat and watched the final minute slip away.

The "what ifs" ran through my mind for years
Never knowing if we would have succeeded
It is like a small part of me is frozen in time
And all those vivid dreams still rage in me.

October 29, 2011

Tiny Green Leaf

A tiny green leaf had lodged into my front hood
As I pulled out of the parking lot one summer's day
The leaf stood tall and straight like it had eyes on me
As my car sped madly down the back country road.

I turned on the pace as I connected with a highway
Moving faster into the night with the leaf flapping
The noise turned into a whistle as it fought to stay put
And I noticed the leaf had not broken a single thread.

My face turned red from the beating noise of the leaf
As my mind had decided I should stop and set it free
My car came to a rolling stop and I slowly got out
I approached the tiny friend who captured my imagination.

I pulled the leaf out and it blew in my hand from the wind
For I was about to release it back to nature's doom
When I noticed the face of a person embedded on it
A dark skull and the eyes and face of someone dear.

I felt the eyes of another were directly looking at me
A feeling of a spirit that had left earlier in my youthful life
Only to fall back into the hands of someone who remembered
So I carefully took the green leaf and tucked it in my pocket.

That one leaf opened up some part of me that had died
A voice came from within and opened up this world to me
I felt like the prayers of thousands had been answered
And to this day I shall consider this one leaf my blessing.

October 29, 2011

The Shack on the Hill

Since boyhood I envisioned it standing there
Built by the efforts of my own imagination
One day I could climb the back hill to find
A place to escape, a place to call my own.

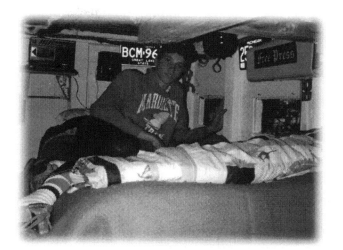

For one year I put that dream into motion
I hauled driftwood with a little red wagon
Built the front door with screws and nails
And found some old carpeting in a garage.

I collected old lumber pieces from a neighbor
As I waited to find a large piece for the roof
I climbed the steep hill to deliver every piece
The day's building never seemed to end.

I used blue paint to make the room expand
Adding some small windows in the front
To take in the blue image of Lake Superior
And the glowing sunrises of early morning.

I remember spending my first night alone
Leaves shaking by the hundreds from above
As an early rain fell from the darkening sky
And I kept warm under a thick layer of covers.

I had given my father the ultimate promise
That if I ever moved away I would take it down
To give nature a chance to return to normalcy
And to let go of a proud childhood memory.

The hammer easily pulled out the first set of nails
Wood pieces were flying and sliding down the hillside
It took one full day to remove a year of youthful effort
But the shack upon the hill still lives in my memories.

October 30, 2011

The Fountain of Youth

There are few things in life that truly mystify
A place where water flows and lights glimmer
For many still believe the legend and the lore
That somewhere stands the fountain of youth.

To step naked inside the round shaped circle
You can extend a life beyond the living years
Youthful energy rushing through your veins
As the forbidden blessing prolongs your life.

Some shall scour the countryside in the hunt
Knowing someone gifted has the directions
To find the place where time seems to stop
And finally bathe in the blessed, sacred water.

But some believe you cannot live beyond fate
To live beyond the destiny of your own birth
You are meddling with the natural balance
A value held deeply in God's vision and soul.

October 30, 2011

True Love

Let me take your hand and we shall fly away
Carry you on my shoulders across the sea
You can trust me; you give me strength
Nothing is impossible when you are near
A long life together with compassion and love.

We shall see the world's beautiful places
And will share in the visions of our dreams
For love can carry us to the highest mountains
You and I will live this life on our own terms
Guided by a tender breeze and our free spirits.

For only true love can show us the meaning
On an Earth that is filled with billions of lost souls
You and I were fortunate to find one another
All those empty roads and failed chances overturned
For one day I will be forever lost in your arms.

We shall be blessed to live every minute together
A beautiful melody played for the whole world
Never missing a single beat in the walk of life
Every day a holiday of giving and endless loving
To raise us to a higher ground until the end of time.

October 30, 2011

Two Trucks

I found myself following behind a red semi
One that hauls garbage across the state line
A whole load of unwanted items being recycled
Finding a new home somewhere in the Midwest.

A thought crossed my mind about waste
The amount we consume and throw away
The number of trucks it takes to haul junk
And the efforts to save Earth from neglect.

Another semi came from the other direction
Carrying new products and valuables to sell
A moment later the two trucks crossed paths
As I saw the vision of a never-ending struggle.

It seems for each good thing we can save
Means another will suffer and fall to the side
The trucks will keep on trucking the material
And the people will keep on buying the goods.

But we live in a time where we over splurge
A generation that forgets how to save a little
To stretch something to the bitter, bitter end
We are consumers who have no way to stop.

If our lives could take care of the smaller ideals
We could rid the Earth of selfish carelessness
And we would not need as many trucks to carry
The mound of trouble we brought on ourselves.

October 31, 2011

One More Year

I knew of this open back office where I worked
A small cubical room with one glass door
And I kept thinking how I could work there
To make an honest living in such a small space.

But I turned that thought into my passion
To begin a life with no promises, no guarantees
My family expressed lots of concern and worry
That being an entrepreneur was a dead end.

I forged through phone books to find a service
That no other business offered on a local basis
And that was when I came across "consulting"
A word that would take twenty years to perfect.

I took on that tiny one-room office for one year
Where the phone hardly rang once a week
And I kept learning computers by trial and error
Putting together the skills that built the foundation.

Day-by-day I struggled to make new business
But each job's success brought in more calls
And I connected with more and more businesses
My belief system said that I could make it a success.

After the year concluded and all bills were paid
I had tallied just $300 dollars in a final net gain
Many would have walked away and cashed out
I wanted to see if I could make it *one more year*.

That optimistic attitude lead to many working years
In a time when people needed help and knowledge
The clients and the problems motivated me to keep learning
And I went on to teach thousands how to use a computer.

I found my passion in becoming a computer consultant
On the cutting edge of technology and new breakthroughs
Using imagination, patience, energy, and my personality
The dreams of being one entrepreneur have come true.

November 1, 2011

Articulate Leader

There is one less leader in our world now
The light went out early on his glowing spirit
He left us with the touches of pure simplicity
Taking technology and making it accessible.

The masses will be following his ideals forever
We honor him daily by using a phone or computer
His intimate touches live on in these products
And his life will be studied for decades to come.

Steve Jobs' unique success cannot be duplicated
Many will try to follow in the footsteps he left behind
But truly gifted innovators seldom come along
The public patiently waits for another one like him.

He arrived at a time when ingenuity sold ideas
The energy to push engineers to the final brink
Like he knew his time on Earth would soon end
Made these products more special, more alluring.

The master planner, salesman, and articulate leader
His life will be known by every human soul on this Earth
His legacy is cemented in the minds of future scholars
A generation that shall continue building his dream.

November 1, 2011

Focus

Do not let your mind wander too far from the path
For you have given so much time and willful effort
To get this far on the longest journey ever taken
Focus has taken you to this exact moment in time.

You can study each move you are about to make
Foreseeing what might happen to you down the line
And you can push yourself beyond mental abilities
Finding yourself one step ahead of everyone else.

The secret is deciding between want and need
Many will let their guard down and wander away
But others will work their lives unraveling the mystery
And learn about the boundaries of their own beliefs.

Having a focus in life gives you the decisive edge
The power to do more, the power to move forward
Nothing can stand in your way in finding success
For your own willpower will keep you well prepared.

November 1, 2011

Alone

I woke up to find myself in a tiny house
Weeping upon the floor in my own tears
A day of firsts and lasts in a young life
For I found myself so terribly alone inside.

Moving out by myself was a test of skill
The decisions yet to be made scared me
My small inner world seemed to collapse
As I came home each night to no one.

We will all find ourselves alone some day
And self-reflection will rule the inner mind
Flowing with emotional pride and concern
As you consider all the promises and regrets.

The world can sometimes be so unforgiving
That you lose some small part of yourself
A part that you never thought had a chance
Returns even stronger and healthier than ever.

The truth stands that we are never really alone
Something carefully watches us from a distance
Our spirits are protected from significant failure
Knowing that someone, somewhere loves us.

November 2, 2011

Five Minutes

Somewhere in the night I shall find you
A ghostly image that you can almost touch
To see your face and hear your laugh again
Would erase all the suffering I have carried.

Just five minutes with you is all I need
To tell you how frustration ruled the years
And the love I had held back from everyone
For I felt you had punished and deserted me.

I could tell you how my story had turned out
How I left behind a single life for a noble marriage
Inspired by children who made me a better man
And not to be lost anymore in a barren world.

You would hear me talk about my passions and fears
Nothing would be off limits to someone like yourself
I have held back these feelings for too many years
I would have one chance to set the record straight.

My whole life has been scarred by your departure
I cried so many nights in desperate need of your help
I wanted to know why you left me behind without a word
Maybe you were planning to come back someday.

But I would let you know one thing before you left me
That every decision, right or wrong, I made in this fragile life
That every success and dream I followed and achieved
I have always felt your gentle spirit flowing through my veins.

November 3, 2011

The Coach

The coach must have leadership qualities
Willing, a motivator, a teacher, energetic
Having skillful eyes to measure adjustment
Making the right plan to carry the team.

The coach knows the secrets of the game
How to play, how to win, how to inspire
Through the strength of his vision and rule
He shapes fundamentals with every player.

The coach directs the team along their way
Helping them through slumps and spurts
Moving up and down the bench like a father
He strives to improve, whether winning or losing.

The coach teaches respect and dignity
Watching how players deal with pressure
He always gives calm and experienced advice
Keeping his team in the game until the end.

The coach knows when the game is through
As he greets the opponent he has just faced
Sure that his players have given their best effort
He walks off the floor proud to be their coach.

November 3, 2011

Hollywood Celebrities

The world is full of never-ending celebrities
Some are from movies and day-time dramas
Today's come from hundreds of reality shows
The remainder live forever on the Walk of Fame.

You cannot forget the recording artists of long ago
The voices of singers and starlets gone silent
Leaving behind a wealth of talent and stardom
And a legacy of a treasured, diverse existence.

We are somewhat perplexed by the celebrity
The fame and fortune, the royalty and gossip
To even the stories of how they got the big break
Propelling them into superstardom and success.

The ordinary person desires a deeper connection
So they, too, can live beyond the realms of time
To be immortalized like a former King or Queen
And to have millions visit the place of their birth.

The obsession with Hollywood celebrities lives on
As they convey happiness by using pure imagination
But with each birthday celebration we feel eternal loss
For they left our hearts hungry and minds wanting more.

November 4, 2011

Chasing Dreams

We all have immense visions in this life
They come in countless shapes and forms
Living inside our waiting and hopeful hearts
And we can only find it by chasing dreams.

Each day brightens along our endless journey
That we might find a unique, simple reply
Leading us to a lifetime of happiness and joy
As we complete the full circle of our lives.

For dreams are hidden treasures out of reach
They hide at the end of stunning rainbows
To be found only by avid, enthusiastic seekers
As the world continues to revolve and grow.

At certain times we feel alone, desolate, needy
The open sky looks like it will never share again
And provide true blessings to an innocent soul
But our chances improve with an open mind.

Even if we do not fulfill our lifelong dreams
We should be proud that we saw the light
And tried with every ounce to chase it down
Closer to the hands that supplied the dream.

November 4, 2011

"There are those who look at things the way they are, and ask why... I dream of things that never were, and ask why not?"

Robert F. Kennedy (1925-1968)

12256887R00049

Made in the USA
Charleston, SC
23 April 2012

With today's technology on the rise, Brian Maki, an Upper Michigan author and poet, takes us back to the finer things in life. Using short stories and poems, he describes the world of The Innocent and Ordinary Life we have lost touch with in the past twenty years. He describes themes like nature, loss, marriage, death, celebrities, love, rainbows and dreams. The book includes a few tales about the trials and tribulations as a veteran basketball official.

Brian always pushes the reader to consider the true life that is going on and to not miss out on it. A wonderful array of thoughts and insights is what makes this book something you can read again and again.

Brian Maki is the author of the 1993 classic "Flying a Kite," a Northern Michigan University graduate, a veteran basketball coach and referee, a private business owner, and an Adult Education Computer Instructor. He has published various prose and poetry pieces in national publications over the years.

ISBN 9781468105827

9 781468 105827

9000